This Journal Belongs To
THE Phenomenal:

_____

Remarkable
Exceptional
Phenomenal
Awesome
Extraordinary

I Am...

Things I Love About Myself....

_____

_____

_____

_____

_____

_____

_____

_____

_____

_____

_____

_____

My Hopes & Dreams

_____

_____

_____

_____

_____

Phenomenal Affirmations

Date:

Daily Affirmation:

Today, I Get To:

Steps For Success:

Thoughts & Reflections:

Phenomenal Affirmations

Date:

I Am Grateful For:

People I am Grateful For:

Blessings In My Life:

Highlights of My Day:

Plans For Tomorrow:

Thoughts & Reflections:

Date: _____

Today I Am Grateful For....

_____

_____

_____

_____

_____

_____

_____

_____

_____

_____

_____

_____

Lessons I've Learned Today

_____

_____

_____

_____

_____

Phenomenal Affirmations

Date:

Daily Affirmation:_____
_____
_____

Today, I Get To: _____
_____
_____

Steps For Success: _____
_____
_____

Thoughts & Reflections:

Phenomenal Affirmations

Date: _____

I Am Grateful For: _____

_____

_____

People I am Grateful For: _____

_____

_____

Blessings In My Life: _____

_____

_____

Highlights of My Day: _____

_____

_____

Plans For Tomorrow: _____

_____

Thoughts & Reflections:

Date: _____

Today I Am Grateful For....

_____

_____

_____

_____

_____

_____

_____

_____

_____

_____

_____

_____

_____

_____

_____

_____

_____

Lessons I've Learned Today

_____

_____

_____

_____

_____

Phenomenal Affirmations

Date:

Daily Affirmation:_____
_____
_____

Today, I Get To: _____
_____
_____

Steps For Success: _____
_____
_____

Thoughts & Reflections:

Phenomenal Affirmations

Date:

I Am Grateful For: ⎯⎯⎯⎯⎯⎯⎯⎯⎯⎯⎯⎯⎯⎯⎯⎯⎯⎯⎯⎯

_____

_____

People I am Grateful For: ⎯⎯⎯⎯⎯⎯⎯⎯⎯⎯⎯⎯⎯⎯⎯⎯

_____

_____

Blessings In My Life: ⎯⎯⎯⎯⎯⎯⎯⎯⎯⎯⎯⎯⎯⎯⎯⎯⎯⎯

_____

_____

Highlights of My Day: ⎯⎯⎯⎯⎯⎯⎯⎯⎯⎯⎯⎯⎯⎯⎯⎯⎯

_____

_____

Plans For Tomorrow: ⎯⎯⎯⎯⎯⎯⎯⎯⎯⎯⎯⎯⎯⎯⎯⎯⎯⎯

_____

Thoughts & Reflections:

Date: _____

Today I Am Grateful For....

_____
_____
_____
_____
_____
_____
_____
_____
_____
_____
_____
_____
_____
_____
_____

Lessons I've Learned Today

_____
_____
_____
_____
_____

Phenomenal Affirmations

Date:

Daily Affirmation:

_____

_____

_____

Today, I Get To: ———————————————

_____

_____

Steps For Success: ———————————————

_____

_____

Thoughts & Reflections:

Phenomenal Affirmations

Date:

I Am Grateful For: —————————————————

_____

_____

People I am Grateful For: ——————————————

_____

_____

Blessings In My Life: —————————————————

_____

_____

Highlights of My Day: ————————————————

_____

_____

Plans For Tomorrow: —————————————————

_____

Thoughts & Reflections:

Date: _____

Today I Am Grateful For....

_____
_____
_____
_____
_____
_____
_____
_____
_____
_____
_____
_____
_____
_____

Lessons I've Learned Today

_____
_____
_____
_____
_____

Phenomenal Affirmations

Date:

Daily Affirmation:_____
_____
_____

Today, I Get To: _____
_____
_____

Steps For Success: _____
_____
_____

Thoughts & Reflections:

Phenomenal Affirmations

Date:

I Am Grateful For: ——————————————————————

———————————————————————————————————

———————————————————————————————————

People I am Grateful For: ————————————————————

———————————————————————————————————

———————————————————————————————————

Blessings In My Life: ——————————————————————

———————————————————————————————————

———————————————————————————————————

Highlights of My Day: ——————————————————————

———————————————————————————————————

———————————————————————————————————

Plans For Tomorrow: ——————————————————————

———————————————————————————————————

Thoughts & Reflections:

Date: _____

Today I Am Grateful For....

_____
_____
_____
_____
_____
_____
_____
_____
_____
_____
_____
_____

Lessons I've Learned Today

_____
_____
_____
_____
_____

Phenomenal Affirmations

Date:

Daily Affirmation:_____
_____
_____

Today, I Get To: ——————————————————————
_____
_____

Steps For Success: ——————————————————————
_____
_____

Thoughts & Reflections:

Phenomenal Affirmations

Date:

I Am Grateful For: ⎯⎯⎯⎯⎯⎯⎯⎯⎯⎯⎯⎯⎯⎯⎯⎯⎯⎯⎯
_____
_____

People I am Grateful For: ⎯⎯⎯⎯⎯⎯⎯⎯⎯⎯⎯⎯⎯⎯⎯⎯
_____
_____

Blessings In My Life: ⎯⎯⎯⎯⎯⎯⎯⎯⎯⎯⎯⎯⎯⎯⎯⎯⎯⎯
_____
_____

Highlights of My Day: ⎯⎯⎯⎯⎯⎯⎯⎯⎯⎯⎯⎯⎯⎯⎯⎯⎯
_____
_____

Plans For Tomorrow: ⎯⎯⎯⎯⎯⎯⎯⎯⎯⎯⎯⎯⎯⎯⎯⎯⎯⎯
_____

Thoughts & Reflections:

Date: _____

Today I Am Grateful For....

_____
_____
_____
_____
_____
_____
_____
_____
_____
_____
_____
_____
_____
_____

Lessons I've Learned Today

_____
_____
_____
_____
_____

Phenomenal Affirmations

Date:

Daily Affirmation:

_____

_____

_____

Today, I Get To:

_____

_____

_____

Steps For Success:

_____

_____

_____

Thoughts & Reflections:

Phenomenal Affirmations

Date:

I Am Grateful For: _____

_____

_____

People I am Grateful For: _____

_____

_____

Blessings In My Life: _____

_____

_____

Highlights of My Day: _____

_____

_____

Plans For Tomorrow: _____

_____

Thoughts & Reflections:

Date: _____

Today I Am Grateful For....

_____

_____

_____

_____

_____

_____

_____

_____

_____

_____

_____

Lessons I've Learned Today

_____

_____

_____

_____

Phenomenal Affirmations

Date:

Daily Affirmation:_____

_____

_____

Today, I Get To: _____

_____

_____

Steps For Success: _____

_____

_____

Thoughts & Reflections:

Phenomenal Affirmations

Date:

I Am Grateful For: _____

_____

_____

People I am Grateful For: _____

_____

_____

Blessings In My Life: _____

_____

_____

Highlights of My Day: _____

_____

_____

Plans For Tomorrow: _____

_____

Thoughts & Reflections:

Date: _____

Today I Am Grateful For....

_____
_____
_____
_____
_____
_____
_____
_____
_____
_____
_____
_____
_____
_____

Lessons I've Learned Today

_____
_____
_____
_____
_____

Phenomenal Affirmations

Date:

Daily Affirmation:
_____
_____
_____

Today, I Get To: _____
_____
_____

Steps For Success: _____
_____
_____

Thoughts & Reflections:

Phenomenal Affirmations

Date:

I Am Grateful For: ——————————————————————
_____
_____

People I am Grateful For: ———————————————————
_____
_____

Blessings In My Life: ————————————————————
_____
_____

Highlights of My Day: ———————————————————
_____
_____

Plans For Tomorrow: ————————————————————
_____

Thoughts & Reflections:

Date: _____

Today I Am Grateful For....

_____
_____
_____
_____
_____
_____
_____
_____
_____
_____
_____
_____

Lessons I've Learned Today

_____
_____
_____
_____

Phenomenal Affirmations

Date:

Daily Affirmation:

Today, I Get To:

Steps For Success:

Thoughts & Reflections:

Phenomenal Affirmations

Date: _____

I Am Grateful For: _____
_____
_____

People I am Grateful For: _____
_____
_____

Blessings In My Life: _____
_____
_____

Highlights of My Day: _____
_____
_____

Plans For Tomorrow: _____
_____

Thoughts & Reflections:

Date: _____

Today I Am Grateful For....

_____
_____
_____
_____
_____
_____
_____
_____
_____
_____
_____
_____
_____
_____
_____

Lessons I've Learned Today

_____
_____
_____
_____
_____

Phenomenal Affirmations

Date:

Daily Affirmation:

Today, I Get To:

Steps For Success:

Thoughts & Reflections:

Phenomenal Affirmations

Date:

I Am Grateful For: ─────────────────────────────

_____

_____

People I am Grateful For: ───────────────────────

_____

_____

Blessings In My Life: ──────────────────────────

_____

_____

Highlights of My Day: ─────────────────────────

_____

_____

Plans For Tomorrow: ───────────────────────────

_____

Thoughts & Reflections:

Date: _____

Today I Am Grateful For....

_____
_____
_____
_____
_____
_____
_____
_____
_____
_____
_____

Lessons I've Learned Today

_____
_____
_____
_____
_____

Phenomenal Affirmations

Date:

Daily Affirmation:_____
_____
_____

Today, I Get To: _____
_____
_____

Steps For Success: _____
_____
_____

Thoughts & Reflections:

Phenomenal Affirmations

Date:

I Am Grateful For: ————————————————————————

_____

_____

People I am Grateful For: ———————————————————

_____

_____

Blessings In My Life: ————————————————————————

_____

_____

Highlights of My Day: ————————————————————————

_____

_____

Plans For Tomorrow: ————————————————————————

_____

Thoughts & Reflections:

Date: _____

Today I Am Grateful For....

_____
_____
_____
_____
_____
_____
_____
_____
_____
_____
_____
_____
_____

Lessons I've Learned Today

_____
_____
_____
_____

Phenomenal Affirmations

Date:

Daily Affirmation:

Today, I Get To:

Steps For Success:

Thoughts & Reflections:

Phenomenal Affirmations

Date:

I Am Grateful For: _____
_____
_____

People I am Grateful For: _____
_____
_____

Blessings In My Life: _____
_____
_____

Highlights of My Day: _____
_____
_____

Plans For Tomorrow: _____
_____

Thoughts & Reflections:

Date: _____

Today I Am Grateful For....

_____
_____
_____
_____
_____
_____
_____
_____
_____
_____
_____
_____
_____
_____
_____

Lessons I've Learned Today

_____
_____
_____
_____
_____

Phenomenal Affirmations

Date:

Daily Affirmation:_____
_____
_____

Today, I Get To : _____
_____
_____

Steps For Success: _____
_____
_____

Thoughts & Reflections:

Phenomenal Affirmations

Date:

I Am Grateful For: ———————————————————————
_____
_____

People I am Grateful For: ———————————————————
_____
_____

Blessings In My Life: ————————————————————————
_____
_____

Highlights of My Day: ————————————————————————
_____
_____

Plans For Tomorrow: ———————————————————————
_____

Thoughts & Reflections:

Date: _____

Today I Am Grateful For....

_____
_____
_____
_____
_____
_____
_____
_____
_____
_____
_____
_____
_____

Lessons I've Learned Today

_____
_____
_____
_____
_____

Phenomenal Affirmations

Date:

Daily Affirmation:

_____

_____

_____

Today, I Get To:

_____

_____

_____

Steps For Success:

_____

_____

Thoughts & Reflections:

Phenomenal Affirmations

Date:

I Am Grateful For: —————————————————————————
_____
_____

People I am Grateful For: —————————————————————
_____
_____

Blessings In My Life: ————————————————————————
_____
_____
_____

Highlights of My Day: ————————————————————————
_____
_____

Plans For Tomorrow: —————————————————————————
_____

Thoughts & Reflections:

Date: _____

Today I Am Grateful For....

_____
_____
_____
_____
_____
_____
_____
_____
_____
_____
_____
_____
_____
_____

Lessons I've Learned Today

_____
_____
_____
_____
_____

Phenomenal Affirmations

Date:

Daily Affirmation:_____
_____
_____

Today, I Get To: _____
_____
_____

Steps For Success: _____
_____
_____

Thoughts & Reflections:

Phenomenal Affirmations

Date:

I Am Grateful For: ——————————————————————

_____

_____

People I am Grateful For: ——————————————————

_____

_____

Blessings In My Life: ———————————————————————

_____

_____

Highlights of My Day: ———————————————————————

_____

_____

Plans For Tomorrow: ————————————————————————

_____

Thoughts & Reflections:

Date: _____

Today I Am Grateful For....

_____
_____
_____
_____
_____
_____
_____
_____
_____
_____
_____
_____
_____
_____

Lessons I've Learned Today

_____
_____
_____
_____
_____

Phenomenal Affirmations

Date:

Daily Affirmation:_____
_____
_____

Today, I Get To: _____
_____
_____

Steps For Success: _____
_____
_____

Thoughts & Reflections:

Phenomenal Affirmations

Date:

I Am Grateful For: _____

_____

_____

People I am Grateful For: _____

_____

_____

Blessings In My Life: _____

_____

_____

Highlights of My Day: _____

_____

_____

Plans For Tomorrow: _____

_____

Thoughts & Reflections:

Date: _____

Today I Am Grateful For....

_____
_____
_____
_____
_____
_____
_____
_____
_____
_____
_____
_____
_____

Lessons I've Learned Today

_____
_____
_____
_____
_____

Phenomenal Affirmations

Date:

Daily Affirmation:_____
_____
_____

Today, I Get To: _____
_____
_____

Steps For Success: _____
_____
_____

Thoughts & Reflections:

Phenomenal Affirmations

Date:

I Am Grateful For: ─────────────────────────
_____
_____

People I am Grateful For: ─────────────────────
_____
_____

Blessings In My Life: ──────────────────────
_____
_____

Highlights of My Day: ─────────────────────
_____
_____

Plans For Tomorrow: ──────────────────────
_____

Thoughts & Reflections:

Date: _____

Today I Am Grateful For....

_____
_____
_____
_____
_____
_____
_____
_____
_____
_____
_____
_____
_____
_____
_____

Lessons I've Learned Today

_____
_____
_____
_____
_____

Phenomenal Affirmations

Date:

Daily Affirmation:_____
_____
_____

Today, I Get To:_____
_____
_____

Steps For Success:_____
_____
_____

Thoughts & Reflections:

Phenomenal Affirmations

Date:

I Am Grateful For: ───────────────────────────
_____
_____

People I am Grateful For: ─────────────────────
_____
_____

Blessings In My Life: ─────────────────────────
_____
_____

Highlights of My Day: ─────────────────────────
_____
_____

Plans For Tomorrow: ───────────────────────────
_____

Thoughts & Reflections:

Date: _____

Today I Am Grateful For....

_____

_____

_____

_____

_____

_____

_____

_____

_____

_____

_____

Lessons I've Learned Today

_____

_____

_____

_____

Phenomenal Affirmations

Date:

Daily Affirmation: _____
_____
_____

Today, I Get To: _____
_____
_____

Steps For Success: _____
_____
_____

Thoughts & Reflections:

Phenomenal Affirmations

Date:

I Am Grateful For:

People I am Grateful For:

Blessings In My Life:

Highlights of My Day:

Plans For Tomorrow:

Thoughts & Reflections:

Date: _____

Today I Am Grateful For....

_____
_____
_____
_____
_____
_____
_____
_____
_____
_____
_____
_____
_____
_____
_____
_____
_____

Lessons I've Learned Today

_____
_____
_____
_____
_____

Phenomenal Affirmations

Date:

Daily Affirmation:
_____
_____
_____

Today, I Get To: _____
_____
_____

Steps For Success: _____
_____
_____

Thoughts & Reflections:

Phenomenal Affirmations

Date:

I Am Grateful For: _____
_____
_____

People I am Grateful For: _____
_____
_____

Blessings In My Life: _____
_____
_____

Highlights of My Day: _____
_____
_____

Plans For Tomorrow: _____
_____

Thoughts & Reflections:

Date: _____

Today I Am Grateful For....

_____
_____
_____
_____
_____
_____
_____
_____
_____
_____
_____
_____

Lessons I've Learned Today

_____
_____
_____
_____
_____

Phenomenal Affirmations

Date:

Daily Affirmation:_____
_____
_____

Today, I Get To: ———————————————————————
_____
_____

Steps For Success: ———————————————————————
_____
_____

Thoughts & Reflections:

Phenomenal Affirmations

Date:

I Am Grateful For:

People I am Grateful For:

Blessings In My Life:

Highlights of My Day:

Plans For Tomorrow:

Thoughts & Reflections:

Date: _____

Today I Am Grateful For....

_____
_____
_____
_____
_____
_____
_____
_____
_____
_____
_____
_____
_____
_____

Lessons I've Learned Today

_____
_____
_____
_____
_____

Phenomenal Affirmations

Date:

Daily Affirmation:

Today, I Get To:

Steps For Success:

Thoughts & Reflections:

Phenomenal Affirmations

Date:

I Am Grateful For: —————————————————————————

People I am Grateful For: —————————————————————

Blessings In My Life: ——————————————————————

Highlights of My Day: ——————————————————————

Plans For Tomorrow: ——————————————————————

Thoughts & Reflections:

Date: _____

Today I Am Grateful For....

_____
_____
_____
_____
_____
_____
_____
_____
_____
_____
_____
_____
_____

Lessons I've Learned Today

_____
_____
_____
_____
_____

Phenomenal Affirmations

Date:

Daily Affirmation:_____
_____
_____

Today, I Get To: _____
_____
_____

Steps For Success: _____
_____
_____

Thoughts & Reflections:

Phenomenal Affirmations

Date:

I Am Grateful For: _____

_____

_____

People I am Grateful For: _____

_____

_____

Blessings In My Life: _____

_____

_____

Highlights of My Day: _____

_____

_____

Plans For Tomorrow: _____

_____

Thoughts & Reflections:

Date: _____

Today I Am Grateful For....

_____
_____
_____
_____
_____
_____
_____
_____
_____
_____
_____
_____
_____

Lessons I've Learned Today

_____
_____
_____
_____
_____

Phenomenal Affirmations

Date:

Daily Affirmation:_____
_____
_____

Today, I Get To: _____
_____
_____

Steps For Success: _____
_____
_____

Thoughts & Reflections:

Phenomenal Affirmations

Date:

I Am Grateful For: _____

_____

_____

People I am Grateful For: _____

_____

_____

Blessings In My Life: _____

_____

_____

Highlights of My Day: _____

_____

_____

Plans For Tomorrow: _____

_____

Thoughts & Reflections:

Date: _____

Today I Am Grateful For....

_____
_____
_____
_____
_____
_____
_____
_____
_____
_____
_____
_____

Lessons I've Learned Today

_____
_____
_____
_____
_____

Phenomenal Affirmations

Date :

Daily Affirmation:_____
_____
_____

Today, I Get To : ——————————————————
_____
_____

Steps For Success: ——————————————————
_____
_____

Thoughts & Reflections:

Phenomenal Affirmations

Date:

I Am Grateful For: —————————————————————————

People I am Grateful For: —————————————————————

Blessings In My Life: —————————————————————————

Highlights of My Day: —————————————————————————

Plans For Tomorrow: —————————————————————————

Thoughts & Reflections:

Date: _____

Today I Am Grateful For....

_____
_____
_____
_____
_____
_____
_____
_____
_____
_____
_____
_____
_____
_____

Lessons I've Learned Today

_____
_____
_____
_____
_____

Phenomenal Affirmations

Date:

Daily Affirmation:

_____

_____

_____

Today, I Get To:

_____

_____

_____

Steps For Success:

_____

_____

_____

Thoughts & Reflections:

Phenomenal Affirmations

Date:

I Am Grateful For: _____
_____
_____

People I am Grateful For: _____
_____
_____

Blessings In My Life: _____
_____
_____

Highlights of My Day: _____
_____
_____

Plans For Tomorrow: _____
_____

Thoughts & Reflections:

Date: _____

Today I Am Grateful For....

Lessons I've Learned Today

Phenomenal Affirmations

Date:

Daily Affirmation:

_____

_____

_____

Today, I Get To: _____

_____

_____

Steps For Success: _____

_____

_____

Thoughts & Reflections:

Phenomenal Affirmations

Date:

I Am Grateful For:

People I am Grateful For:

Blessings In My Life:

Highlights of My Day:

Plans For Tomorrow:

Thoughts & Reflections:

Date: _____

Today I Am Grateful For....

_____

_____

_____

_____

_____

_____

_____

_____

_____

_____

_____

_____

_____

_____

Lessons I've Learned Today

_____

_____

_____

_____

_____

Phenomenal Affirmations

Date:

Daily Affirmation:
_____
_____
_____

Today, I Get To: _____
_____
_____

Steps For Success: _____
_____
_____

Thoughts & Reflections:

Phenomenal Affirmations

Date:

I Am Grateful For: ⎯⎯⎯⎯⎯⎯⎯⎯⎯⎯⎯⎯⎯⎯⎯⎯
_____
_____

People I am Grateful For: ⎯⎯⎯⎯⎯⎯⎯⎯⎯⎯⎯⎯⎯
_____
_____

Blessings In My Life: ⎯⎯⎯⎯⎯⎯⎯⎯⎯⎯⎯⎯⎯⎯⎯
_____
_____

Highlights of My Day: ⎯⎯⎯⎯⎯⎯⎯⎯⎯⎯⎯⎯⎯⎯
_____
_____

Plans For Tomorrow: ⎯⎯⎯⎯⎯⎯⎯⎯⎯⎯⎯⎯⎯⎯⎯
_____

Thoughts & Reflections:

Date: _____

Today I Am Grateful For....

_____
_____
_____
_____
_____
_____
_____
_____
_____
_____
_____

Lessons I've Learned Today

_____
_____
_____
_____
_____

Phenomenal Affirmations

Date:

Daily Affirmation:_____
_____
_____

Today, I Get To: _____
_____
_____

Steps For Success: _____
_____
_____

Thoughts & Reflections:

Phenomenal Affirmations

Date:

I Am Grateful For: ———————————————————————

_____

_____

People I am Grateful For: ———————————————————

_____

_____

Blessings In My Life: ——————————————————————

_____

_____

Highlights of My Day: ——————————————————————

_____

_____

Plans For Tomorrow: ———————————————————————

_____

Thoughts & Reflections:

Date: _____

Today I Am Grateful For....

_____
_____
_____
_____
_____
_____
_____
_____
_____
_____
_____
_____
_____
_____

Lessons I've Learned Today

_____
_____
_____
_____
_____

Phenomenal Affirmations

Date:

Daily Affirmation:

Today, I Get To:

Steps For Success:

Thoughts & Reflections:

Phenomenal Affirmations

Date:

I Am Grateful For: _____

_____

_____

People I am Grateful For: _____

_____

_____

Blessings In My Life: _____

_____

_____

Highlights of My Day: _____

_____

_____

Plans For Tomorrow: _____

_____

Thoughts & Reflections:

Date: _____

Today I Am Grateful For....

_____

_____

_____

_____

_____

_____

_____

_____

_____

_____

Lessons I've Learned Today

_____

_____

_____

_____

Phenomenal Affirmations

Date:

Daily Affirmation: _____
_____
_____

Today, I Get To: _____
_____
_____

Steps For Success: _____
_____
_____

Thoughts & Reflections:

Phenomenal Affirmations

Date:

I Am Grateful For: _____
_____
_____

People I am Grateful For: _____
_____
_____

Blessings In My Life: _____
_____
_____

Highlights of My Day: _____
_____
_____

Plans For Tomorrow: _____
_____

Thoughts & Reflections:

Date: _____

Today I Am Grateful For....

_____
_____
_____
_____
_____
_____
_____
_____
_____
_____
_____
_____
_____
_____

Lessons I've Learned Today

_____
_____
_____
_____
_____

I Am...

Made in the USA
Columbia, SC
12 May 2023

16596463R00057